Murder World

UNSOLVED

The Alphabet

Killer

Contents

Introduction

Agatha Christie's 1936 novel *The ABC Murders* is a classic of crime fiction. Detective Hercule Poirot seeks a serial killer who seems to choose his victims based only on their alliterative initials and the town or city in which they live. Alice Ascher is killed in Andover, then Betty Barnard dies in Bexhill before Sir Carmichael Clarke is murdered in Churston....

Of course, in real life murderers don't choose their victims using such neat literary devices. Or do they?

In Rochester County, New York, between 1971 and 1973, three young girls were abducted, sexually assaulted, strangled and their bodies dumped close to busy roads. The body of ten-year-old Carmen Colón was found close to the village of Churchville. Eighteen months later, the body of eleven-year-old Wanda Walkowicz was found next a busy road in the town of Webster. Seven months after that the body of eleven-year-old Michelle Maenza was discovered on a rural road in the small town of

Macedon. Police sought a single killer but these crimes remain unsolved.

Can this really be true? Is this simply an outrageous coincidence or did a deranged serial killer choose his young victims based on nothing more than the fact that their Christian and surnames began with the same letter? Did he then deliberately leave their bodies to be discovered in towns that also began with the same letter?

Bizarre and contrived though it sounds, this isn't fiction. This is the strange, unsettling but true story of the murderer who became known as the Alphabet Killer.

Part 1: The Murders

In the early 1970s, the city of Rochester in Monroe County, New York was not a place generally associated with violent crime. Urban renewal had led to the creation of new malls and city-centre public areas. New high-rise commercial buildings such as the Xerox Tower provided accommodation for many banks and legal firms.

This was a prosperous city and if it was known for anything in particular, beyond being the location for the corporate headquarters for Eastman Kodak, it was for jazz. The jazz clubs on Clarissa Street became famous as the most popular location in upstate New York to watch some of the biggest stars of the genre.

All of which made the events of Tuesday, November 16th, 1971 not just horrifying but very difficult to understand.

Chapter 1: 1971

Carmen Colón

At around 4:30pm in the afternoon of Tuesday November 16th, 1971, ten-year-old Carmen Colón went to Jax Pharmacy on West Main Street, in the downtown area of Rochester, on the west side of the Genessee River. Petite, brunette Carmen was not able to speak English fluently. She had been born in Rochester but had spent most of the first half of her life living in her native Puerto Rico. In

1966, the family: Carmen, her siblings, her father Justiniano and her mother Guillermina, had moved back to Rochester. However, her parents had separated and Guillermina and the children moved into an apartment on Romeyn Street. Soon after, Guillermina began a relationship with Justiniano's brother Miguel, known by the Colón children as Uncle Miguel.

Carmen's grandparents lived in a house on Brown Street, just ten-minutes' walk away from her home. Carmen often spent time at her grandparent's home and, by November 1971, was living there almost permanently while her mother, sisters and a new stepsister born nine months before, remained with Uncle Miguel in the apartment on Romeyn Street.

Carmen was a bright and happy child, though she did suffer from recurring nightmares that were so bad that they occasionally caused her to fall out of bed in panic. She attended John Williams School No. 5 in Rochester but she struggled in several subjects. The problem wasn't her intelligence or willingness to work but her lack of English. The school lacked the resources to provide dual language tuition and Carmen had been placed in several Special Education classes to help her catch up.

On Tuesday 16th November, Guillermina visited Carmen and her mother and father-in-law at the house on Brown Street. Her nine-month old child was ill and she urgently needed a prescription to be picked up from a pharmacy on the corner of West Main and Genessee Streets. Carmen immediately offered to pick up the prescription for her mother.

She had done this in the past, but always while accompanied by her grandfather, Felix Colón. On this occasion, she begged to be allowed to go alone. It was only a short walk from the house to the shopping plaza in which the pharmacy was located, so it was agreed that Carmen could undertake the errand on her own while her mother waited in the house on Brown Street. Carmen left her grandparent's home at around 4:30pm.

When she arrived at the pharmacy a few minutes later, she was told that it would take around half an hour to prepare the prescription. She said that she couldn't wait and that she would return. She went outside and it was at this point that a witness saw her get into a car. Another witness on the street outside noted that Carmen was taken by the arm and ushered into the car by a man, though she said that there didn't appear to be a struggle and the girl did not seem at all distressed.

By 5:00pm, it was beginning to get dark and the Colón family were getting worried about the fact that Carmen had not yet come home. A family member was sent out to the pharmacy look for her, but he soon returned without having seen her. Other family members also looked for Carmen but when they too failed to find her, the Colón family reported her missing to the Rochester Police Department at around 7:00pm. What they didn't know was that a very odd and disturbing occurrence had already been seen by a number of witnesses on Interstate 490, one of the main expressways in the city of Rochester.

It was around 5:15pm and rush hour traffic was building on the stretch of Interstate 490 known as the Western Expressway, near Exit 3 to Churchville. Passing commuters saw a young girl, naked from the waist down, running along the side of the freeway in the gathering darkness. She seemed to be fleeing from a car that was reversing towards her on the hard shoulder. She was obviously distressed, waving and shouting frantically, but no-one stopped or called the police. Police would later estimate that at least 100 vehicles must have passed the girl as she ran along the side of the busy road.

Two days later, two teenagers cycling on Steams Road near the village of Churchville, less than 10 miles west of Rochester, saw what they at first thought was a "*broken doll.*" Police arrived and found the body of Carmen Colón in a field close to Interstate 490. She was wearing only a sweater, socks and sneakers. Her coat was found around 100 feet from her body.

An autopsy revealed that she had been raped and manually strangled, but she also had a number of other injuries including a fractured skull, broken vertebrae and many small scratches and abrasions on her body. It was assumed that some of these injuries might have been caused when her killer tossed her body into the field from the freeway above, possibly from a moving car.

Two weeks later her trousers, crumpled and frozen, were found in a field less than 200 feet from Interstate 490 and close to where Carmen had been seen running at the side of the road.

On 22nd November, Carmen Colón was buried in Holy Sepulchre Cemetery in Rochester after a funeral service at St. Peter and Paul's Roman Catholic Church.

Chapter 2: 1973

Wanda Walkowicz

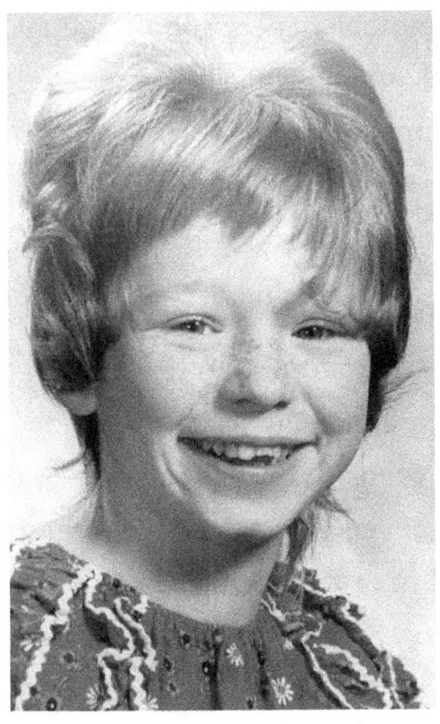

In some ways, eleven-year-old Wanda Walkowicz was very different to Carmen Colón. Red-haired and blue-eyed, she was a feisty tomboy who was more likely to be found kicking a football with the boys than playing with girl's toys. However, like Carmen, she was part of a relatively poor Catholic family in a rundown area of inner Rochester. Her father had died a few years before and Wanda and her sisters, ten-year-old Rita and two-year-old Michelle, lived with their mother, Joyce in an apartment in north-central Rochester. Wanda had been having problems at school, struggling to perform well in any subject. But in late March 1973, she brought home a report card that showed clear signs of improvement. Her mother was so delighted that she planned to frame the report card and hang it on the wall.

Wanda and her sister Rita often did odd jobs in the neighbourhood, helping to clean neighbour's houses and tending their yards. One of the errands she most enjoyed was going to a local delicatessen after school to collect shopping for her mother. The store was on Conkey Avenue, a short distance from Wanda's home and just three miles from the pharmacy on West Main Street that Carmen Colón had visited just before she disappeared nearly eighteen months before.

At around 5:00pm on Monday 2nd April 1973, Wanda left her home to go to the delicatessen to pick up shopping. When three hours had passed and Wanda had not returned, her mother reported her missing to the Rochester Police Department.

Police visited the delicatessen and discovered that Wanda had been there, made her purchases at around 5:20pm and then left. Around 50 police officers searched the area close to the store and places where Wanda was known to have played. They could not find any sign of the missing girl.

The following day, a state trooper, Thomas Zimmer, pulled his vehicle into a rest area on State Route 104, around five miles east of Rochester and within the small town of Webster. On an embankment close to the rest area he saw a girl's body. The search for Wanda Walkowicz was over.

An autopsy showed that she had been raped and strangled from behind with a ligature, possibly a belt. She had several other injuries that suggested that she had fought her attacker. It appeared that she had been re-dressed after the attack and, just like Carmen Colón, it also appeared that her body had been tossed on to the embankment from a moving vehicle. Numerous strands of white cat hair were found on her clothes and body. However, it also seemed that Wanda had eaten less than one hour before her death, something that must have happened after her abduction. The autopsy noted the presence of a "*custard-like*" food in her stomach.

Wanda Walkowicz joined Carmen Colón in Holy Sepulchre Cemetery on 6th April 1973, after a funeral service at St. Michael's Church on Clinton Avenue.

Michelle Maenza

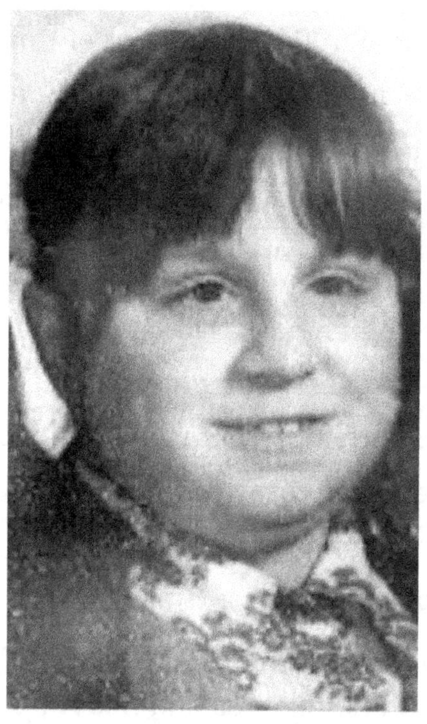

Eleven-year-old Michelle Maenza lived in a house on Webster Crescent in a rundown area of Rochester around one mile east of the Genesee

River. Her parents were separated and Michelle lived with her mother, Carolyn, and her two younger sisters. Her two brothers lived separately with their father, Christopher.

Michelle attended school at John James Audubon School 33 at 500 Webster Avenue. Like the previous victims, she was struggling at school, not academically, but because she was the target of bullying. She was carrying a little extra weight, which made the other girls pick on her and taunt her. On Monday November 26th 1973, seven months after the abduction and murder of Wanda Walkowicz, Michelle had spent much of the afternoon at school in the nurse's office, crying. She was extremely upset as the other girls had been particularly cruel to her that day. When school ended, she walked home. Her mother often came to collect her and walk home with her, but on this particular day, Michelle walked home alone.

The journey from school to her home covered just half a mile and should have taken Michelle no more than fifteen minutes. Two other girls from her school saw her at around 3:20pm, close to Webster Avenue and only a few minutes from the school.

Michelle never arrived at her home. After a brief search, her mother called to report her missing to the Rochester Police Department.

Around forty police officers immediately began searching for Michelle. They searched the area between the school and her home and stopped cars to ask drivers if they had seen her. There were no other sightings and no trace of Michelle.

Two days later, Michelle's body was discovered in a ditch on Eddy Road, a rural road in Macedon, a small town around five miles south-east of Rochester. Her body was fully clothed. She had been raped and strangled from behind with a ligature thought to have been a rope. Her corpse was covered in small bruises. A forensic examination of semen found on her body suggested that she had been raped by a single individual. A partial palm-print was lifted from her neck. Foliage found in one of her clasped hands matched that of the area where she had been found, suggesting that she had been strangled at the same location.

Soon after, her coat was found around half a mile away, close to Eddy Road. Police surmised that her killer had forgotten to dump her coat, and had tossed it from his car when he noticed it as he drove away.

On December 1st 1973, after a funeral service at Corpus Christi Church, Michelle Maenza was also buried in the Holy Sepulchre Cemetery.

Chapter 3: Other Murders

Only three murders have been attributed to this killer: those of Carmen Colón, Wanda Walkowicz and Michelle Maenza. However, a murder occurred in Rochester in 1976 that fuelled fears that the Alphabet Killer might have struck again. Seven-year-old Michelle McMurray lived with her mother, Deborah Ruggles, in an apartment in Jay Street in Rochester. Deborah left her daughter sleeping in the apartment between 02:00 and 03:00am on 11th April. When she returned, Deborah found that her daughter was missing. She immediately called the police.

A search quickly located Michelle's body in a driveway close to the apartment. She had been raped and strangled. The press was filled with speculation that this was another murder committed by the Alphabet killer, but the police were certain that it was not. Although they did not release details, they noted that the sexual assault on Michelle McMurray was significantly different, leading them to believe that she had been murdered by a different killer.

Despite an intensive investigation at the time, no-one was charged with Michelle McMurray's murder. Thirty-one years later, new evidence was uncovered that led investigators to James Pressler, a man who had been employed as the superintendent in the building in which the McMurrays had lived. A DNA sample was obtained from Pressler and this was found to match samples on Michelle McMurray's body. Pressler was charged with second-degree murder in 2007 but he died of a heart-attack in a Florida prison before he could face trial. It was found that his DNA did not match the sample found on Wanda Walkowicz's body and other evidence made it clear that he could not be the alphabet killer.

Investigators believe that no other murders in the greater Rochester area have been committed by the Alphabet Killer.

Chapter 4: November 1971 – April 1973

When the press learned details of the murder of Carmen Colón, and particularly the fact that the young girl had been seen fleeing from her killer by the side of Interstate 490, but that no-one stopped to help or even to see what was happening, there was outrage in Rochester. Two local newspapers, *The Times-Union* and the *Democrat and Chronicle* combined to offer a reward of $2,500 for information leading to an arrest. Local businesses in Rochester increased this to $6,000 (worth around $40,000 today) soon after.

Another local business, the Rochester Outdoor Advertising Company, donated the use of five large billboards next to expressways in the city. Each featured an eight-foot high picture of Carmen under a headline that read: *Do You Know Who Killed Carmen Colón?* The billboards also noted the reward and provided a telephone number created by Rochester Police Department specifically for members of the public to provide information on this murder.

Hundreds of people called the anonymous *"Secret Witness Line."* Some were commuters who had seen Carmen running by the side of Interstate 490. All said that they had not stopped because the freeway was very busy, it was almost dark and it was raining and they considered that stopping might have been dangerous. Most also said that they had assumed that someone else would do something about the frightened child. *"I felt that someone behind me was in a better position to help"* was one fairly typical comment.

One of these witnesses described seeing what seemed to be the same girl being led submissively back to the vehicle which was parked on the hard shoulder, though they were not able to provide a description of the man or the vehicle. Some of these witnesses told police that they believed that the vehicle they had seen reversing behind the girl was a dark-coloured Ford Pinto hatchback, though none were able to give a description of the driver. Other witnesses described a completely different car. Of the six witnesses who contacted the witness line there did not seem to be any agreement on the make or even the colour of the vehicle.

However, though none of the tips produced any new leads, Rochester police already had a suspect in mind for this murder, Carmen's uncle, twenty-four-year-old Miguel Colón. After Carmen's parents separated, Miguel had begun a relationship with her mother, Guillermina. Miguel owned a car similar to the one described by one of the people who had called the witness line describing the vehicle seen at the side of Interstate 490. Even more interesting to police, another anonymous caller claimed that Miguel had abruptly moved back to Puerto Rico less than one week after the murder after allegedly saying that he had "*done something wrong in Rochester.*"

Miguel was extradited back to Rochester in March 1972 to face questioning, but he denied all involvement in the murder and police were not able to find any direct evidence to charge him. He was released in April 1972. (You'll find more information about the main suspects in this case in Part 3 of this book).

Despite the lack of hard evidence, it seems certain that the police were initially convinced that Miguel Colón was responsible for the murder of Carmen Colón. A number of other leads were followed up, but none led to the identification of any other viable suspects.

There was a brief flurry of interest when a Californian man was arrested for the rape and murder of a young girl in early 1972. When he was arrested, he was found to have in his wallet a photograph of Carmen Colón, clipped from a newspaper report of her murder. But further investigation proved that this man had been serving with US forces in Vietnam in November 1971, meaning that he could not have been Carmen's murderer.

Chapter 5: April 1973 – November 1973

After days of questioning potential witnesses, Police investigating the abduction and murder of Wanda Walkowicz were able to find several people who might have seen her as she walked home from the delicatessen. Several residents remembered seeing her walking north on Avenue B with her bag of groceries. Three schoolmates saw her in the same area, stopping to brace her bag of groceries against a fence as she struggled to get a better grip. These girls also recalled seeing a brown car driving slowly past. When they looked back a little later, both Wanda and the brown car had vanished.

One other witness recalled seeing Wanda standing next to a stationery brown car just a few hundred yards from her home, apparently talking with the driver. This witness did not see the driver and was not able to recall the make of the vehicle. Soon after the discovery of her body, posters featuring a photograph of Wanda were placed on utility poles and in stores in the area in which she had last been seen. These posters were bilingual (in English and

Spanish) and noted that a $10,000 reward was being offered for information that led to an arrest. The posters also included the telephone number for a new anonymous secret witness line.

Police received over two hundred calls, but only two seemed to offer positive new evidence. A woman said that she had seen a red-haired girl she believed to have been Wanda being dragged into a light-coloured Dodge Dart car on Conkey Avenue between 5:30 and 6:00pm on the evening that she had gone missing. She didn't give her name and because the line was anonymous, police were unable to contact this witness to follow-up on this alleged sighting.

Another female caller also reported seeing a light-coloured Dodge Dart car near the rest area where Wanda's body was discovered. Again, police were unable to contact this woman to follow-up, but residents in the area in which Wanda had disappeared were warned to look out for this type of vehicle. Police also spoke with Wanda's mother who told them that, two days before she was abducted, Wanda and a nine-year-old friend had been walking near a railroad line close to their home when the girls had been frightened by a man, lurking in bushes and who seemed to be following them. The other girl's mother had called police to report the incident, but neither girl had got a good look at the man and they were not able to provide a description of him.

Other police enquiries also identified two ten year-old-girls who claimed that they had been followed by a man driving a 1971 Ford LTD who had tried to persuade them to get into the car. Both had been frightened by the experience and told their parents. As this happened just a few days before Wanda was abducted and in the same general area, their parents contacted the Rochester Police Department. Police spoke to the girls who provided what seemed to be a good description of the man. He was around 5 feet and ten inches tall, about thirty years of age, he had a black beard and a distinctive mole on his forehead. He was wearing a long black coat.

Soon after, police identified a local man who closely matched this description. He was questioned for more than ten hours but, after he passed a lie-detector test and provided a verifiable alibi for the time of Wanda's abduction and murder, he was released without charge.

In September 1973, a local television station, WOKR, broadcast a 30-minute reconstruction of Wanda's disappearance and the discovery of her body. This led to more calls to the Witness Line, but none generated significant new leads.

The autopsy on Wanda identified semen and pubic hair on her body and noted that she had been redressed after death. One intriguing fact that emerged from the autopsy was that several strands of white cat hair were found on Wanda's body and clothing. The Walkowicz family did own a cat, but it did not have white hair.

After months of investigation, the Rochester Police Department were making little progress on identifying Wanda's killer. They one thing that they were certain about, and which they repeated on more than one occasion to the press, was that there was no connection between this murder and the earlier murder of Carmen Colón. Given the obvious similarities, that seems odd but, eight months later, the murder of Michelle Maenza would force them to reconsider this view.

Chapter 6: November 1973 - present

For the first time, these three murders were formally linked by Rochester Police. Detective lieutenant Anthony Fantigrossi told a press conference after the discovery of Michelle's body:

> *"The man who killed Wanda Walkowicz is responsible for this murder. There's a strong possibility that he's also responsible for killing Carmen Colón."*

The press began to refer to this unknown serial killer as the *Double-Initial Killer* and then by the name by which he is best remembered, the *Alphabet Killer*. There was intense speculation about his motives and whether the fact that all three victims had double initials was coincidence or part of a bizarre pattern.

The police investigation into the murder of Michelle Maenza began in the same way as the two previous investigations, with the posting of advertisements asking for information, noting that a reward was available for information leading to an arrest and providing the number of a new anonymous witness line.

Many calls were received, though only a few offered useful new leads. One witness claimed to have seen a tan coloured car with a young girl in the passenger seat travelling at high speed on Ackerman Street at around 3:30pm, around ten minutes after Michelle was last seen walking on Webster Avenue, a short distance away. This witness believed that the girl might have been Michelle and noted that she appeared to be crying.

The most significant lead came from a woman who had seen a girl whom she believed to have been Michelle at a Carrols Drive-in Restaurant at Panorama Plaza in the town of Penfield at around 4:30pm. Penfield is around two miles east of Rochester and approximately mid-way between the area where Michelle lived and the town of Macedon where her body was later found. The girl had been with a man who seemed to be taking a carry-out order back to a vehicle.

This was particularly significant because the autopsy on Michelle's body found that she had eaten a meal of hamburger and onions around one hour before she died. That meant that she must have eaten the meal after she had been abducted, though this was not widely known at the time. This witness was able to provide a detailed description of the man she had seen. He was Caucasian, aged between 25 and 35, around six feet tall and slim with dark hair that fell over his face and dark stubble on his cheeks. He was wearing a ski jacket, plaid shirt and jeans tucked into cowboy boots with buckles at the top. She did not see what type of vehicle the man was driving.

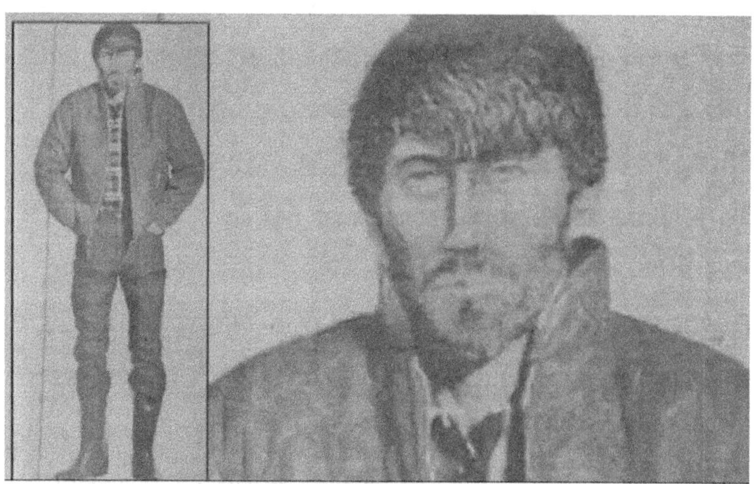

A police composite image of the man seen with a girl at the Carrols Drive-in Restaurant in Penfield.

Another witness told police that he had been driving on Route 350 in the town of Walworth (around four miles north of Macedon) at around 5:30 when he seen a light-coloured vehicle stopped at the side of the road. Believing that it might have a flat tyre, he slowed to see if the driver needed help. As he approached, he could see that the driver, who was standing next to the car, was holding a young girl by the wrist. He pushed the girl behind him and out of sight. As the driver cruised slowly by, he said that the man shook his fist and glared at him with such an angry and menacing expression that he decided not to stop. The description given by this witness was less complete than that of the woman who had seen a man and girl outside the restaurant in Penfield, but it was sufficiently similar that it could have been the same man.

This witness came back to talk to police few days later. During the original sighting, he had been able to see part of the licence number of the car stopped at the side of Route 350. A few days later, he saw the same car and driver and this time he was able to get the complete license number. This information led police to the owner of the car, an unemployed petty criminal living with his family in the town of Lyons, around fifteen miles east of Rochester.

This man resembled the description given by the witness at the drive-in restaurant and he was taken in for questioning. He denied any involvement in Michelle's abduction or murder and told police that he had spent the day at home, job hunting. A check of phone records seemed to support this and the man's family confirmed that he had been at home at the time that Michelle vanished. The man, who has never been identified, passed a lie detector test and was released without charge.

A composite sketch was created by police artists based on the descriptions of witnesses and widely distributed in the area. Several suspects who matched this description were questioned, but all were released without charge. All possible leads were investigated but none led to the identification of a new suspect.

Then, on January 1st 1974, a man committed suicide after being pursued by police after attempting to abduct a young girl in Rochester. He was twenty-five-year-old Dennis Termini, a firefighter who worked for the city Fire Department.

Subsequent investigation made him a major suspect in the three murders, though it now seems unlikely that he was the killer (see Chapter 8 for more information on Dennis Termini).

In 2009 the *Democrat and Chronicle* newspaper published a series of articles on these murders and on the police investigation. These articles resulted in the Rochester Police department receiving more than twenty calls that opened new lines of enquiry. All were followed up but none led to the identification of any new suspects.

Part 3: The Main Suspects

During the forty-year investigation into the Alphabet Murders, a number of suspects have been identified. Most were quickly ruled out. This section provides a brief overview of the main suspects in this case.

Chapter 7: Miguel Colón

Soon after the murder of Carmen Colón, an anonymous caller used the secret witness line to identify Miguel Colón as a potential suspect. The caller noted that Miguel had fled back to Puerto Rico a few days after the murder, and added that Miguel had said that he had to leave the US because he had "*done something wrong in Rochester.*" Unsurprisingly, Puerto Rican Miguel Colón quickly became the main suspect in this case.

Miguel had been involved in a relationship with Carmen's mother after she had separated from his brother, Justiniano. He knew the Colón children well and was known to them as "*Uncle Miguel.*" Enquiries confirmed that he had left the US for Puerto Rico on 21st November 1971, four days after the murder. He had left behind his car, which wasn't a Ford Pinto, but was visually similar to that model. When police looked at the vehicle, they found that the interior had been recently cleaned and the trunk had been treated with some form of chemical agent. A visit to the dealership where Miguel had purchased the car a few weeks before the murder, revealed that it had not been cleaned in this way before it was sold. Inside the car police found a doll that was said by Carmen's mother to have belonged to her daughter.

In March 1972, detectives from Rochester Police Department travelled to San Juan in Puerto Rice to question Miguel. They discovered that Miguel had left the city. It looked as though he was trying to avoid talking to investigators, but a few days later, he turned himself in to the authorities in San Juan. He agreed to be extradited back to Rochester where he was questioned extensively by investigators.

Miguel was unable to provide an alibi for his whereabouts at the time of the murder, though he vehemently denied any involvement. He was given a lie-detector test by police officials, and this seemed to confirm that he was telling the truth. He explained the presence of Carmen's doll in the car by telling police that Carmen and the other Colón children often rode in his car. This was confirmed by Guillermina and Miguel claimed, reasonably, that the doll must have been left in his car sometime in the past.

He also told police that he had not fled from San Juan to avoid talking to investigators from Rochester, but had gone to another area to visit a sick aunt. This was also found to be true. With a complete lack of any physical evidence to link him to the crime and a lie-detector test that seemed to confirm that he was telling the truth, police were left with no option but to release Miguel Colón.

After his release, Miguel Colón moved back to Rochester. In 1991 he was married and living in an apartment in Radio Street. After an altercation during which he shot and wounded both his wife and brother-in-law, police were called. When they arrived, Miguel first told police to shoot him and when they refused, shot himself and died at the scene.

After his death investigators talked with members of his family to ask whether he had ever confessed to Carmen's murder or said anything that might implicate him. Almost everyone questioned denied this and claimed to believe that Miguel had no involvement in Carmen's murder.

In 1995, Carmen Colón made her first public statement when she gave an interview to the

Democrat and Chronicle newspaper. In the interview, she said that if she could be granted one wish before her death, it would be to know who killed her daughter. This strongly suggests that she did not believe that Miguel Colón was her daughter's killer.

Chapter 8: Dennis Termini

In 1st January 1975, five weeks after the murder of
Michelle Maenza, a man attempted to abduct a
teenage girl in Rochester at gun point. The girl's
screams led to the man fleeing and police were
called. While they were still attending this incident,
police received another call, this time from a
woman who had seen a man with a gun drag a
young girl into a garage.

Police went to the location, and a man carrying a
gun fled from the scene. Initially, police lost him
before two officers tracked him to parked car. As
they waited for back-up, the man shot himself in
the head. By the time police reached the vehicle,
he was dead.

Subsequent investigation revealed that the man
was twenty-five-year-old Dennis Termini, a
firefighter with the Rochester Fire Department. It
also appeared that he was a serial rapist operating
in Rochester who had become known as the
"*garage rapist.*" Between 1971 and 1973, he was
suspected of carrying out fourteen rapes of girls
and women in the Rochester area. However, there

were several links that seemed to make him a viable suspect in the Alphabet Murders.

He owned a beige car similar to that seen by some witnesses. When his car was examined, white cat hairs were found on the seats and carpet. In the car, Termini kept his firefighter's uniform. Police speculated that he have used that to reassure the young girls and lure them into his car. Finally, he lived in an apartment on Bock Street, just a few blocks from Michelle Maenza's school.

All these things made Termini seem to be a viable suspect, though all the known victims of the garage rapist were 18 or older and Termini had no history of sexual molestation of children. The matter was partly resolved in 2007 when Termini's body was exhumed in order to take a sample for DNA analysis. By that time, only the samples taken from Wanda Walkowicz were still suitable for testing, but the results were conclusive. Termini had not raped Wanda Walkowicz. Given that police were certain that Michelle Maenza and Wanda had been raped and killed by the same man, this also seemed to make it certain that he was not responsible for either of those murders and there was no evidence to connect him to the murder of Carmen Colón.

Dennis Termini is no longer considered a suspect in these murders.

Chapter 9: Joseph Naso

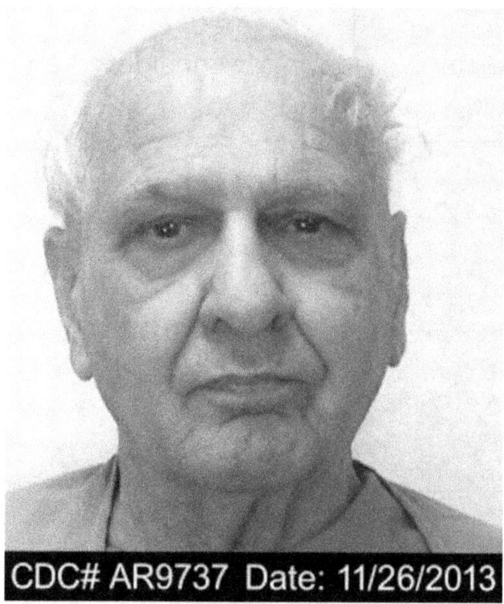

In 2010, seventy-six-year-old Joseph Naso was arrested on parole violation charges. He had a long history of petty crime including shoplifting that continued even while he was in his seventies. His arrest led to a police search of his home in Reno, Nevada and that led to the discovery of a handwritten diary that seemed to connect Naso with a number of unsolved murders.

In 2011 he was charged with the murders of four women:

- 18-year-old Roxenne Roggasch in 1977

- 22-year-old Carmen Colón in 1978
- 38-year-old Pamela Parsons in 1993
- 31-year-old Tracy Tafoya in 1994

The fact that all four victims had names with the same initials in their first and last names inevitably led to speculation that Naso might also be connected with the murders in New York in 1972-1974. This interest grew when it was learned that Naso, who was originally from New York, might have spent time living Rochester during the 1970s, though it proved difficult to define precisely when and he had mainly lived in California at that time.

He would have been 38 at the time of the Alphabet Murders and he was 5' 11" tall with dark hair, making him sufficiently similar to the police composite image of the man seen with Michelle Maenza to be of interest as a suspect (though his dark hair was thinning by that time, making it unlikely that it would have fallen over his face in the way described by the witness who saw this man). But, other than the fact that all four of Naso's victims had double initials and that he might have spent time in Rochester, there was really nothing to connect Naso with the other three Alphabet Murders in New York.

All four of Naso's victims were adult sex workers. He was later charged with two additional murders of sex workers, and neither of those victims had double initials and none were children. Naso's diary suggests that he often didn't know the names of his victims and was unaware of the fact that four of them had double initials.

Naso's diary also appeared to describe the murder of several other women though, to date, these victims have not been identified. Naso was tried in 2013 in Marin County for all four murders. He chose to represent himself at the trial and denied responsibility for any of the murders. He was found guilty on all counts of on August 20th, 2013. He was subsequently sentenced to death and is currently incarcerated in California. It seems unlikely that he will live long enough to be executed. The death sentence has been in abeyance in California since 2006 and there are hundreds of prisoners on death row in that state.

Any possible connection between Joseph Naso and the murders in New York was finally disproved when, after his conviction, samples from his victims in California were compared with DNA samples from Wanda Walkowicz. This confirmed that the person who had raped Wanda was not Joseph Naso.

Chapter 10: Tik-Tok Grandfather

In April 2022, a woman posted a short video on Tik-Tok in which she claimed that her grandfather may have been the Alphabet Killer. The clip quickly attracted more than half a million views with many people urging the woman to take her suspicions to the police.

Later the same month, newspaper reports identified the woman as a Rochester resident, 21-year-old Alexis Ortiz. She explained that her grandfather had worked in a store in Conkey Avenue at the time that Wanda Walkowicz went missing. She also claimed that her grandmother and grandfather knew Wanda's family and that both had met Wanda. Her grandfather (who has not been named) did not own any cats, but there were cats in the store in which he worked.

She said that the rumour that her grandfather had been the Alphabet Killer was often discussed within the family. Her grandfather was said to have claimed to have spoken to Wanda on the day she went missing. He was also said to have been one of the first to offer a reward when her body was found in Webster, though some family members claimed that he seemed to know that this was Wanda even before the identity of the body was announced by police. He also resembled the composite image released by police of the man last seen with Michelle Maenza and he was questioned by police during the initial investigation but released without charge.

This man moved to Las Vegas in the 1980s, breaking all contact with his family and children. He died in 2020. The Ortiz family contacted police after the release of the viral Tik-Tok video. A DNA sample was taken from one of the man's daughters. To date, Rochester Police Department have not released the results of DNA testing.

Chapter 11: Kenneth Bianchi

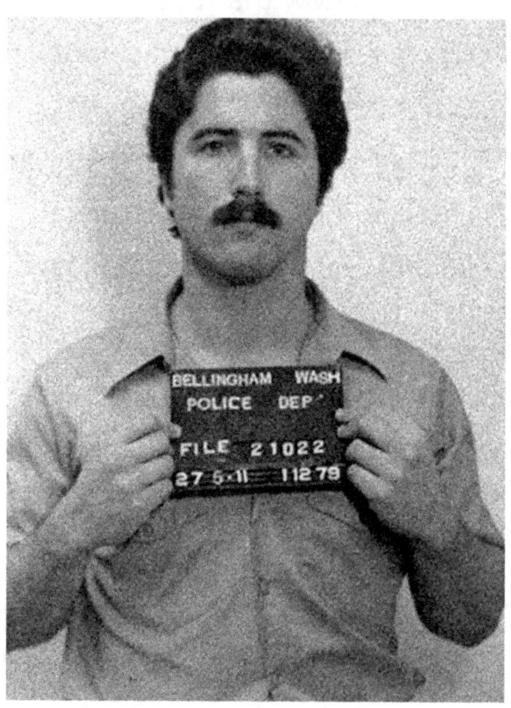

In 1979, two men, Kenneth Bianchi and his cousin Angelo Buono, were arrested in Los Angeles on suspicion of abducting, raping and murdering at least twelve girls and young women in California and Washington State. The pair, who became known as the Hillside Stranglers, were both tried, convicted and sentenced to life imprisonment.

Angelo Buono died in September 2002 in Calipatria State Prison. Bianchi is currently serving his sentence in Washington State Penitentiary in Walla Walla. He will not be eligible for parole until 2025.

Almost as soon as he was arrested, Bianchi became a suspect in the Alphabet Murders. He was born in Rochester and grew up in that city where he was raised by adoptive parents. He moved to Los Angeles in 1976. Angelo Buono was also born in Rochester but he moved to Los Angeles in 1939, when he was five years old.

Bianchi vehemently denies any involvement in the Alphabet murders and has even asked police to clear his name and remove him from the list of suspects. However, there were aspects of the killings committed by the Hillside Stranglers that seemed similar to the Alphabet Murders.

Most of the victims of the Hillside Stranglers were adults, but the youngest was just twelve-years-old. Bianchi has also written in prison about how he enjoyed sex with girls as young as eleven. Most of the victims of Bianchi and Buono were abducted, raped and strangled and their bodies dumped next to roads. This was also true of the victims of the Alphabet Killer: the bodies of all three victims could easily have been hidden, but instead they were left where they would be quickly found.

After his conviction, Bianchi's adoptive mother Francis made a perceptive comment, noting that Bianchi was unable to handle any form of rejection. She also pointed out that many of the murders in California and Washington State were committed following a rejection of Bianchi by a girlfriend or after the loss of a job.

Bianchi suffered several significant rejections during the period 1971 – 1973. In 1972, at the age of 21, he applied for a position with Monroe County Sherriff's Department, having completed one year of a course on police science and psychology at Monroe Community College in Rochester. His application was rejected. He married (for the second time) in 1972, but his wife left him after nine months. In the period 1970 – 1973, he proposed several times to a woman he had known since he was 18, but she turned him down each time because he did not have a stable job.

In the period 1972 – 1974, he worked on several occasions as a security guard, but he was dismissed more than once when it was discovered that he had been stealing from the premises he was employed to guard.

At the time of the murders, Bianchi had a part-time job working as an ice-cream vendor in Rochester and was known to have worked in locations close to where two of the victims disappeared. He also owned a light-coloured car similar to the vehicle described by some witnesses and he looked similar to the composite image produced by police artists of the man last seen with Michelle Maenza. In 1972 he wrote a letter to another girlfriend in which he claimed that he was a suspect in the Alphabet Murders, though this does not seem to have been true at that time. The woman to whom he sent the letter did not believe him.

All these factors made Bianchi a strong suspect in the Alphabet Murders, but DNA analysis proved that he was not the man who raped Wanda Walkowicz. Despite this, Rochester Police investigators have not ruled out the possibility that he was involved in the Alphabet Murders in some way and he remains a person of interest in this case.

Chapter 12: Conclusion

The first thing to consider in this case is whether Carmen Colón, Wanda Walkowicz and Michelle Maenza were all killed by the same person?

Even leaving aside the fact that all had double-initial names and that all were dumped in towns that shared the same initial, the similarities are certainly striking:

- All three were pre-adolescent girls from relatively poor, single-parent Catholic families.
- All three were relatively small for their age.
- All were suffering from some degree of social isolation. Carmen Colón due to her lack of English, Wanda Walkowicz due to her poor performance at school and Michelle Maenza due to bullying. This isolation might have made all of these victims vulnerable to a *"friendly"* predator offering treats such as food.
- All were abducted in a relatively small area of downtown Rochester.

- All were abducted on weekdays in the downtown area of Rochester, in the late afternoon and on days when it was or had been raining.
- One of the victims (Carmen Colón) was seen to get into a car, seemingly willingly, with her abductor. Neither of the other two seem to have screamed or called out, which implies that they too may have initially gone with their abductor willingly.
- All three were raped and strangled.
- No attempt was made to hide any of the bodies. All three were dumped next to busy roads and in locations where they were likely to be found quickly.

However, there are also some significant differences that must be considered:

- Carmen Colón was manually strangled. The other two victims were strangled from behind using a ligature.
- Carmen Colón's body was found partially clothed. The other two bodies were fully dressed, but both had been re-dressed after death.

- White cat hairs were found on Wanda Walkowicz's body and clothes. Similar hairs were not found on the bodies of either of the other two victims.
- The autopsies on Wanda Walkowicz and Michelle Maenza indicated that both had eaten after they had been abducted. Carmen Colón did not eat after her abduction.

Where does that leave us? The murders of Wanda Walkowicz and Michelle Maenza are certainly very similar and it seems reasonable to conclude that they were most likely committed by the same person. There are differences between these and the first murder of Carmen Colón, but might that be simply because the killer became more adept at the process of abduction and murder and modified his approach? Looking at the physical evidence, it seems almost certain that two of these murders were committed by a single killer and possibly all three.

Is it possible to use the science of criminal profiling to help assess whether all three may have been killed by the same person?

Robert Ressler is one of the founder members of the FBI Behavioral Science Unit, the agency that first developed criminal profiling. Ressler analysed the Alphabet Murders and concluded that Wanda Walkowicz and Michelle Maenza were killed by the same person while Carmen Colón was most probably murdered by someone else.

The reasons for this conclusion included Ressler's deduction that the murder of Carmen Colón showed a significantly higher level of anger (which Ressler claimed suggested that she was killed by someone she knew) and that he believed that the two latter murders indicated a higher level of intelligence. Ressler's final summary was that Carmen Colón's killer was known to her and was most likely a man aged 25-30, with low to average intelligence, alcohol abuse problems and an explosive and violent temper. The killer of Wanda Walkowicz and Michelle Maenza, he claimed, was a man of average intelligence who had probably previously committed lesser sexual offences such as exhibitionism and/or making obscene telephone calls.

If we accept Ressler's profile, that certainly suggests two killers and seems to point to Miguel Colón as a likely suspect in Carmen Colón's murder. Unfortunately, criminal profiling is not an exact science and other profilers and criminologists have disagreed, claiming that all three victims were most likely killed by the same person. Author and criminologist Christopher Berry-Dee, for example, claims that he is "*100 per cent*" certain that a detailed analysis of these murders shows that all three murders must have been committed by Kenneth Bianchi.

The police investigation from November 1973 on was certainly based on the assumption that all three murders were committed by the same person. Given that police investigators have access to all the evidence, including details that may not have been made public and despite the claims of Robert Ressler, it does seem reasonable to conclude that there was a single murderer involved.

In terms of a physical description of this killer, the information provided by the witness who saw a man and a girl at the Carrols Drive-in Restaurant in

Penfield at around 4:30pm on the day that Michelle Maenza was abducted seems critical. The timing is certainly plausible. Penfield is around five miles from the centre of Rochester where Michelle was last seen at approximately 3:30pm and half way between Rochester and Macedon where her body was later found. The autopsy showed that Michelle had eaten hamburger and onions less than one hour before her death and that restaurant served hamburger. The description given by this witness and the composite image produced by police artists may be the best information we have about what the Alphabet Killer looked like. This witness described the man as:

> "Caucasian, aged between 25 and 35, around six feet tall and slim with dark hair that fell over his face and dark stubble on his cheeks. Wearing a ski jacket, plaid shirt and jeans tucked into cowboy boots with buckles at the top."

It's also worth thinking for a moment about this sighting and what it tells us the psychology of the murderer if this really was the Alphabet Killer. This man had abducted a young girl less than one hour before and, given that this was not the first killing, he knew that he planned to rape and murder her. Yet he was willing to allow himself to be seen in a public place with his victim. This shows either astonishing confidence or a complete lack of caution.

If this was the killer, he made no attempt to hide or conceal himself or his victim and seems to have been unafraid that he might be seen or identified. Abduction, rape and murder had, it appears, become routine. This also seems to connect with the way in which the bodies of all three victims were disposed of. In each case, these were left in the open, often next to busy roads and in places where they would be quickly found. Any of the bodies could have been hidden, delaying discovery for some time. This killer either didn't care how quickly his victims were found or perhaps actively enjoyed reading about the discovery of the bodies and the police investigation.

These factors suggest an arrogant killer who did not fear identification and arrest. That makes it even harder to understand why the killing of Michelle Maenza would be the last of the Alphabet

Murders. Someone so experienced and confident could have been expected to continue killing but instead, he stopped. Why? Did he leave the area to continue his murders elsewhere? Was he incarcerated? Did he become ill or was he injured? Did some other significant life-change mean that he could no longer spend time stalking and abducting young girls?

What about the main suspects? Miguel Colón was clearly the principal suspect in the initial murder of Carmen Colón. However, he was not the killer of either Wanda Walkowicz or Michelle Maenza. If there was a single murderer in this case, then clearly it cannot have been Miguel Colón. He also passed a lie-detector test while being interviewed by police and there was no physical evidence to connect him with the murder of Carmen Colón.

Both Dennis Termini and Joseph Naso initially looked like good suspects, but DNA testing seems to have proven conclusively that neither of these men was responsible for the murder of Wanda Walkowicz (the only victim from who viable DNA samples are still available). Of course, that does not rule out either of these suspects in the other two murders, but if police are correct and only a single killer was responsible for all three murders, then this could not have been either Naso or Termini.

Tik-Tok Grandfather seems to have been identified as a suspect mainly through family stories. Given that he abandoned his family and had no contact with them, there is bound to be some bad feeling involved, which may account for this accusation. This case is based on hearsay and unsupported speculation and only the completion of DNA analysis will show if it is true.

Which leaves us with Kenneth Bianchi. Bianchi is a convicted multiple murderer whose known victims include a 12-year-old girl (though bizarrely and despite his conviction, Bianchi continues to deny any involvement in the Hillside Strangler murders). DNA analysis seems to prove that Bianchi was not responsible for the rape of Wanda Walkowicz. However, he remains a person of interest in this case.

What is the evidence against Bianchi?

- He is a sexual predator and murderer who is known to have killed one girl of a similar age.
- He was working as an ice-cream vendor in the area where the victims disappeared. This would have allowed him to have contact children who weren't known to him.
- He owned a light-coloured car similar to that described by some witnesses.
- He bears a striking resemblance to the police composite image of a suspect in this case.

Bianchi continues to deny any involvement in these murders and has repeatedly demanded the Rochester Police remove his name from the list of suspects. We know from DNA analysis that he did not rape Wanda Walkowicz, but it is a possibility that he was involved in these murders in some way, perhaps working with a partner as he did in Los Angeles.

Of course, it is also entirely possible that this killer is someone who so far has not come under suspicion.

And what of the elephant in the room? The fact that all three victims had double-initial names and that their bodies were all left in towns that shared the same initial? Was this nothing more than a bizarre coincidence? That seems unlikely, though it isn't completely impossible. When Joseph Naso was originally charged with four murders, the four victims all had the same initials for their first and last names, but there is no evidence that Naso was aware of that or even knew the names of these victims. A coincidence in terms of victim names is certainly possible in the case of the Alphabet Murders, but when you add the fact that all the bodies of three victims in this case were also dumped in towns that started with the same letter, then that seems to be stretching chance occurrence a little too far.

If these victims were chosen partly on the basis of their names, then that does tell us something important about the killer. Specifically, he must have known his victim's names before he abducted them. That means that, however briefly, he must have had some prior contact with all three girls. That's very unusual. Statistics tell us that most children who are murdered are killed either by family members, people they know well or by complete strangers.

In 1973, Dr David Barry, Assistant Professor of Psychiatry at the Rochester Medical School, gave an interview to the New York Times newspaper in which he spoke about the Alphabet Murders. He told the newspaper that he had not come across in his own experience or in the literature of criminal actions based on mental health issues where victims had double initials.

There is no way to assess how many girls in the city of Rochester had double initials in the early 1970s and so no means to calculate the statistical likelihood of three girls chosen at random having double initials. We can say, however, that this is at least unusual and, when combined with the fact that all three victim's bodies were left in towns with the same initial, does strongly suggest that this fact was known to the murderer and somehow significant.

Is there an undiscovered common factor linking all three victims? All were from relatively poor, single-parent families. Two (Carmen Colón and Wanda Walkowicz) were not performing well at school and Michelle Maenza suffered from bullying. It has been suggested that the killer may have been involved with (or had knowledge of) a social services agency in Rochester. This would have given him information about these girl's names and might even have meant that he was known to them and might therefore have been able to gain their confidence and persuade them to get into his car.

Of course, this is no more than conjecture. The killer might also have been employed in a position that gave him access to census data, birth certificates or something similar that would allow him to target victims with double initials. Or, he might have been employed in another role, such as working in a nearby store, that would have allowed him to meet these girls and perhaps to ask them their names. Some prior connection with the victims might also explain why he was able to abduct them from busy streets without anyone noticing. No-one reported any scene that involved a struggle or distressed girl being dragged into a vehicle. It does seem more likely that each victim initially entered the killer's car more-or-less willingly and that strongly suggests a prior connection.

It is also worth returning to the Agatha Christie novel *The ABC Murders*. In that novel (spoiler alert!), the solution is that what seems like an arbitrary series of victims chosen by a serial killer on the basis of their double initials is something quite different. The killer actually wants to murder the third victim, but attempts to hide that murder by making it seem to be part of a random series. Is it possible that one of the victims here was the main target and that the others were killed to disguise that fact?

Or was the murder of Carmen Colón and the dumping of her body in Churchville no more than a coincidence that inspired a different killer to carry out two more murders that were intended to seem to be part of the same series? Both these notions seem unlikely, but the fact of the double initials, the dumping of the bodies in towns with names that begin with the same initial seem to be beyond coincidence. The similarities with the novel *The ABC Murders* is also so striking that it seems very likely that the killer may well have been aware of this work of fiction.

Over to You

You now have the facts of this remarkable and unique case and in the *Further Information* section you'll find additional sources of information. In order to solve this case, there are a number of key questions that must be answered:

- Were all three of these children killed by a single murderer?
- Was the killer aware of the victim's names and were they chosen because of their double initials?
- Were the dump sites chosen because they were towns that began with the same letters as the victim's names or was this no more than a macabre coincidence?
- How were the victims persuaded to get into the killer's vehicle? Did they know their murderer?
- Why did the Alphabet Killer stop after three victims?
- Was the Alphabet Killer one of the suspects identified by investigators?
- If not, who was the Alphabet Killer?

This remains an open case that is still being investigated by Rochester State Police. The presence of testable DNA from Wanda Walkowicz's body means that it would still be possible to positively identify her killer if a new suspect were to be found. But after 50 years, it now seems unlikely that these bizarre and disturbing murders will ever be solved unless some entirely new evidence is discovered or someone is able to suggest a new solution.

If you have <u>any</u> information that you think might help to solve these murders, then please contact Rochester State Police at (585) 398-4100 or email them at crimetip@troopers.ny.gov.

Further Reading

Agatha Christie, *The ABC Murders*, 1936.

Cheri Farnsworth, *Alphabet Killer: The True Story of the Double Initial Murders*, Stackpole Books, 2010.

Emily G. Thompson, *Unsolved Child Murders: Eighteen American Cases, 1956-1998*, Exposit Books, 2017. Includes one chapter on the alphabet murders.

The Alphabet Killer, 2008. A dramatized movie loosely based on the Alphabet murders. Directed by Rob Schmidt and starring Eliza Dushku, Cary Elwes and Timothy Hutton.

Murder World: Unsolved

Have you ever wanted to be a homicide detective?

Then this is the true crime series for you! Each book covers one of the most perplexing unsolved murder cases from around the world. Every case is meticulously researched to bring you all you need to know: the victims, the murders, the timeline, the investigations, the clues and the suspects. The only thing missing is a solution. That's down to you...

Can you do what the investigators couldn't?

Can you analyse the evidence and identify a killer?

Other books in the Murder World: Unsolved series:

The Babysitter: the true story of a sadistic child killer.

February 15th 1976. Ferndale, Michigan. On a cold night a 12 year old boy walks into the darkness and vanishes.

Just another runaway?

But later his dead body is found in a nearby parking lot. He had been bound, smothered and brutally sexually assaulted.

And as more boys and girls vanish, only to be found abandoned, murdered and abused, panic spreads through the community. Police begin a desperate manhunt, but despite witness sightings and trace evidence, the trail stays cold.

Who was the killer and where was he hiding the abducted children?

This is the incredible true story of the search for a serial killer who not only viciously preyed on children, but also fed, bathed and cared for them.

Who was The Babysitter?

Jack the Stripper: the hunt for the prostitute murderer in swinging London

It was 1963 and London was starting to swing...

The Beatles first LP was released, the Great Train Robbery took place and the public read scandalous details of the Profumo Affair involving spies, call girls and MPs.

But a long shadow from Victorian times was falling over the city. Like his famous predecessor, Jack the Ripper, a savage serial killer was murdering prostitutes and dumping their naked bodies in public view. The first corpse was found by the River Thames and was followed by another. And another.

Despite suspects, witness descriptions and forensic evidence, like the police in 1888, law enforcement were baffled as the body count piled high and public pressure grew.

This book tells the incredible true story of the vicious crimes and the desperate hunt for the faceless serial killer who became known Jack the Stripper.☐

Massacre in the Forest: The unsolved 2012 Annecy shootings

On a fine September day in 2012, a lone cyclist sets off for a pleasant ride through the beautiful Combe d'Ire forest in Southern France. Without warning he finds himself in the middle of an unimaginable scene of blood, death and horror.

A dead man lies in the road next to his abandoned bicycle. A car is backed into an earth bank, its engine still running and with three dead occupants. A young girl stands bleeding and battered in front of him. All the dead people have been brutally shot and killed only moments before...

So begins the start of a ten year investigation that crosses countries and continents to discover the perpetrator of the massacre in the forest and find out why the peaceful countryside was shattered by this horrible crime.

This is the full and horrifying story of the Annecy murders.

Join the conversation

We would love to hear your theories, ideas and new information about these true crimes.

And you can stay up to date with the latest news, publications and connect with other true crime fans too.

Twitter

@MURDERWORLD1

Facebook

https://www.facebook.com/justthecrimes